Send an email to "**info@trafficjamming.com**" and write in the subject line, "Promo Code." By doing so, this will allow you to join the "TrafficJamming" Business Family and receive a one-hour consultation on how to grow your customer base. In addition, you will also receive a Free Online Directory Report outlining what your prospects and clients see when searching for your business online (a $197.00 value). To learn more, visit **www.trafficjamming.com**.

Jeff Shavitz on

The Power of Residual Income

You Can Bank on It!

By Jeff Shavitz

THiNK*aha*®

An Actionable Business Journal

E-mail: info@thinkaha.com
20660 Stevens Creek Blvd., Suite 210
Cupertino, CA 95014

⇨ Please pick up a copy of this book on AHAthat and share each AHAmessage socially at http://aha.pub/residualincome.

Published by THiNKaha®
20660 Stevens Creek Blvd., Suite 210, Cupertino, CA 95014
http://thinkaha.com
E-mail: info@thinkaha.com

First Printing: June 2016
Paperback ISBN: 978-1-61699-160-9 (1-61699-160-7)
eBook ISBN: 978-1-61699-161-6 (1-61699-161-5)
Place of Publication: Silicon Valley, California, USA
Paperback Library of Congress Number: 2015950357

Trademarks

All terms mentioned in this book that are known to be trademarks or service marks have been appropriately capitalized. Neither THiNKaha, nor any of its imprints, can attest to the accuracy of this information. Use of a term in this book should not be regarded as affecting the validity of any trademark or service mark.

Warning and Disclaimer

Every effort has been made to make this book as complete and as accurate as possible. The information provided is on an "as is" basis. The author(s), publisher, and their agents assume no responsibility for errors or omissions. Nor do they assume liability or responsibility to any person or entity with respect to any loss or damages arising from the use of information contained herein.

Dedication

To my parents for giving me the support and encouragement to follow my heart and for teaching me the value of being respectful to all human beings. They have taught me to live each day to its fullest. They have been and continue to be my role models on how I want to live my life. Their dedication and loyalty to family is everything.

Acknowledgement

To my father, who introduced me to the industry of payments and credit card processing, my first residual-based business. Without his business direction and advice, I would have never entered the exciting world of residual income.

How to Read a THiNKaha® Book
A Note from the Publisher

The THiNKaha series is the CliffsNotes of the 21st century. The value of these books is that they are contextual in nature. Although the actual words won't change, their meaning will change every time you read one as your context will change. Experience your own "AHA!" moments ("AHAmessages™") with a THiNKaha book; AHAmessages are looked at as "actionable" moments—think of a specific project you're working on, an event, a sales deal, a personal issue, etc. and see how the AHAmessages in this book can inspire your own AHAmessages, something that you can specifically act on. Here's how to read one of these books and have it work for you:

1. Read a THiNKaha book (these slim and handy books should only take about 15–20 minutes of your time!) and write down one to three actionable items you thought of while reading it. Each journal-style THiNKaha book is equipped with space for you to write down your notes and thoughts underneath each AHAmessage.

2. Mark your calendar to re-read this book again in 30 days.

3. Repeat step #1 and write down one to three more AHAmessages that grab you this time. I guarantee that they will be different than the first time. BTW: this is also a great time to reflect on the actions taken from the last set of AHAmessages you wrote down.

After reading a THiNKaha book, writing down your AHAmessages, re-reading it, and writing down more AHAmessages, you'll begin to see how these books contextually apply to you. THiNKaha books advocate for continuous, lifelong learning. They will help you transform your AHAs into actionable items with tangible results until you no longer have to say "AHA!" to these moments—they'll become part of your daily practice as you continue to grow and learn.

As the Chief Instigator of AHAs at THiNKaha, I definitely practice what I preach. I read *Alexisms* and *Ted Rubin on How to Look People in the Eye Digitally*, and one new book once a month and take away two to three different action items from each of them every time. Please e-mail me your AHAs today!

Mitchell Levy
publisher@thinkaha.com

THiNKaha®

Contents

Section 1

Do You Want More Security for Your Company and Yourself?

Whether you are the business owner or the
salesperson, do you want to better your life?
Do you want to earn money while you're sleeping?
Do you want to feel more secure every day?
Here are a few thoughts to ponder.

1

Residual income won't last forever, but work hard to make it last as long as possible. @JeffShavitz

_____

_____

_____

2

Did you go to college and consciously determine your career path? @JeffShavitz

_____

_____

_____

3

If you don't think you're in the right industry, it is never too late to change careers to better your life. @JeffShavitz

_____

_____

_____

4

I love my residual business – you will too!
@JeffShavitz

_____

_____

_____

5

Do you hate the fact that you are always
starting over after each sale? Do you feel
continual pressure to hit your quota?
@JeffShavitz

_____

_____

_____

6

With a salaried job, your earnings are fixed,
except for your subjective bonus.
@JeffShavitz

7

What is active income? Active income is
a direct result of effort. You're a hair stylist
and charge $25.00 per hour. @JeffShavitz

8

Thinking of changing your career?
Consider a residual-based business.
@JeffShavitz

_____

_____

_____

9

Never feel comfortable with your residual income production. Work harder when times are good! @JeffShavitz

_____

_____

_____

10

Your income should be increasing every month – if it's not, find a new job!
@JeffShavitz

_____

_____

_____

11

Control your financial destiny. It stinks to be dependent on others. @JeffShavitz

_____

_____

_____

Section II

What's Your Income? Transactional or Residual?

Entrepreneurs, business owners, and salespeople earn the majority of their income by their sales performance. Is your income based on creating a relationship with a customer and earning a one-time commission? Don't you think you should explore residual income? Read on.

12

Transactional Income Def: The opposite of residual and recurring income. It's one-time! @JeffShavitz

_____

_____

_____

13

A business transaction is quite different than a transactional business. @JeffShavitz

_____

_____

_____

14

Some residual-based industries include credit card processing, insurance, health clubs, and the alarm industry.
@JeffShavitz

_____

_____

_____

15

Some transaction-based industries include doctors, lawyers, food caterers, photographers, and many others. @JeffShavitz

_____

_____

_____

16

Writing a book is a residual-based business: you write it once and then sell the books for the rest of your life. @JeffShavitz

_____

_____

_____

17

Income is very identifiable with a recurring revenue-based business. @JeffShavitz

_____

_____

_____

18

Some multi-level marketing programs are good and some are bad. Do your due diligence and research prior to engaging. @JeffShavitz

_____

_____

_____

19

Residual-based businesses have high
attrition because the salesperson takes
the customer relationship for granted.
@JeffShavitz

_____

_____

_____

20

Daily contact with existing customers is typically minimal with many residual-based businesses. @JeffShavitz

_____

_____

_____

21

As smaller touchpoints are required, delivering exemplary customer service with residual-based businesses is easier. @JeffShavitz

_____

_____

_____

22

Not all revenue is created equal. Understand the value proposition of your product or service. @JeffShavitz

_____

_____

_____

23

Attrition is the worst word in the residual business. Try to avoid it as best as you can! @JeffShavitz

_____

_____

_____

24

There are thousands of network marketing companies to earn residual income. Do your homework to find one to fit your goals.
@JeffShavitz

25

A residual-based business is a "win-win-win" formula. The owner loves it, the salesperson loves it, and the customer loves it.
@JeffShavitz

Section III

Make Money While You Sleep!

Do you want to earn income that allows you to make money while you sleep? Even if it's a nominal amount, it's exciting to have money hitting your bank account while you're focused on other areas of business growth.

26

Residuals are like money in the bank –
actually, they ARE money in the bank.
@JeffShavitz

_____

_____

_____

27

When you're sleeping, wake up, because
something may go wrong! Takes hard
work to make money. @JeffShavitz

_____

_____

_____

28

It all comes down to one word – "Freedom."
I want it and have structured my personal
and professional career around it.
@JeffShavitz

_____

_____

_____

29

Many home-based businesses are
considered residual businesses.
@JeffShavitz

_____

_____

_____

30

Residual income is the perfect way to build wealth for the future, for your family, children, and grandchildren. @JeffShavitz

_____

_____

_____

31

Residual income allows you to make money when you sleep; actually, you can be in a coma and still make money! @JeffShavitz

_____

_____

_____

32

Leverage yourself to earn more than just a hourly wage. Can you? Not every industry can do this. Not with residual income. @JeffShavitz

_____

_____

_____

33

If cash is king, then what are residuals? Residuals are cash's eternal twin. @JeffShavitz

_____

_____

_____

34

Disability insurance is expensive to protect your financial future; I believe residual income is a better form of insurance. @JeffShavitz

_____

_____

_____

35

What is residual income? Read this book http://aha.pub/residualincome. (If you didn't receive a good answer, call me for a refund!) @JeffShavitz

_____

_____

_____

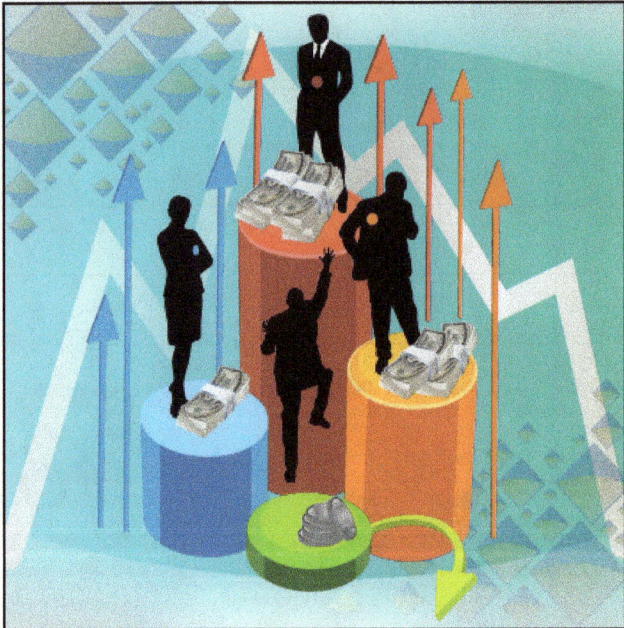

Section IV

Start Reaping the Benefits!

"Work smarter, not harder." Take the stress out of "hoping" for income, and by developing a residual income strategy, you will earn guaranteed revenue in perpetuity.

36

Take the stress out of "hoping" for income – residuals and recurring revenue make financial planning more accurate. @JeffShavitz

_____

_____

_____

37

I can make money when I'm sleeping –
that's so cool. @JeffShavitz

38

Residual income stimulates looking
forward to the end of the pay period.
@JeffShavitz

39

It's fun when the month starts and you know you have "guaranteed" income coming in. @JeffShavitz

_____

_____

_____

40

It's great to go on a vacation and know money is still coming in while you are not working. @JeffShavitz

_____

_____

_____

41

Residual income takes the guesswork out of budgeting. @JeffShavitz

_____

_____

_____

42

Let's highlight the power of the compounding effect of residual income. It's very powerful. @JeffShavitz

_____

_____

_____

43

Your client relationship is the most important aspect of your residual-based business. Never forget that.
@JeffShavitz

_____

_____

_____

44

Being a 1099 contractor provides you the ability to earn income from the client until the end of the working relationship.
@JeffShavitz

_____

_____

_____

45

Work for yourself and take charge of your future income. @JeffShavitz

_____

_____

_____

46

Two types of sales professionals: those who build the brand & business portfolio of someone else & those who build their own. @JeffShavitz

_____

_____

_____

47

If you stick with it, you will make more money tomorrow than you're earning today. That's it. @JeffShavitz

---

48

Major benefit of great client relationships is opportunity to sell them add'l products to earn add'l money. @JeffShavitz

_____

_____

_____

49

Residual-based companies are attractive to potential buyers and demand high multiples because of recurring income streams. @JeffShavitz

_____

_____

_____

50

When was the last time you saw your insurance guy? For that one sale, he gets a slice of your check every time you pay it. @JeffShavitz

_____

_____

_____

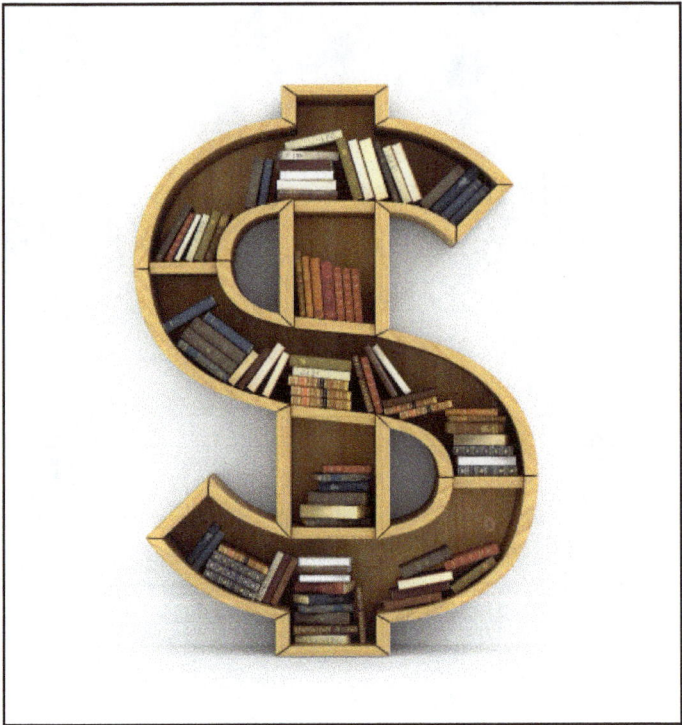

Section V

Business Knowledge Gives You the Power

Business owners and salespeople must understand that knowledge is critical in amassing wealth and value for you and your company. Take control of recurring revenue programs by employing residual income programs.

51

Can you charge money on a continuous, regular basis that clients will month in, month out want to buy from you? @JeffShavitz

_____

_____

_____

52

Having spent 15 years in the merchant services/credit card processing industry, I understand the value of residual income. @JeffShavitz

_____

_____

_____

53

A salesperson should be able to close 10 deals per month, very doable in my industry of payment processing/merchant services.
@JeffShavitz

_____

_____

_____

54

How many clients are necessary for steady & exponential income? What is that called? Passive income, residual income? Bingo!
@JeffShavitz

_____

_____

_____

55

You visit the doctor, who charges you $200 for their time. It's an expensive visit, but they can only charge for time. @JeffShavitz

_____

_____

_____

56

The hardest deal to close in your residual-based business is your first deal! @jeffshavitz

_____

_____

_____

57

Your compensation earnings means the sky is the limit with residual selling vs. a traditional job with a fixed income. @JeffShavitz

_____

_____

_____

58

Understand the compounding nature of residual earnings is powerful. Mo 1 is small; Mo 12 and 24 will be large – I promise. @JeffShavitz

_____

_____

_____

59

At the end of yr 1, business people who work hard and smart will create a solid client base and income. @JeffShavitz

_____

_____

_____

60

Earn $30,000 in year 1 in your residual business; year 5 with same performance will equal $150,000 per year. Not bad. @JeffShavitz

_____

_____

_____

61

Each Dec., review/forecast your "new math" and how many deals are projected to close in the coming year. @JeffShavitz

_____

_____

_____

62

You must understand the math of residual earnings. If you don't, you will give up after a few short months. @JeffShavitz

_____

_____

_____

63

Watching your monthly residual reports increase each month is very powerful for your mind, body, and spirit. @JeffShavitz

_____

_____

_____

64

The customer you just sold your residual service TODAY will help pay for your annual vacation TOMORROW. @JeffShavitz

_____

_____

_____

65

True financial freedom is when your monthly residual earnings are greater than your monthly expenses. @JeffShavitz

_____

_____

_____

66

Create a plan of how many deals to close each month to reach your quota. It could be 1 or 30, depending on your business. @JeffShavitz

_____

_____

_____

67

The power of exponential growth works beautifully with residual income.
@JeffShavitz

_____

_____

_____

68

"One day, my hard work will
earn me a raise & a better life"; rather:
"Every deal I close improves my standard
of living." @JeffShavitz

_____

_____

_____

69

"If you understand residual income, you
would walk through a brick wall to get it."
-Art Jonak, entrepreneur via @JeffShavitz

_____

_____

_____

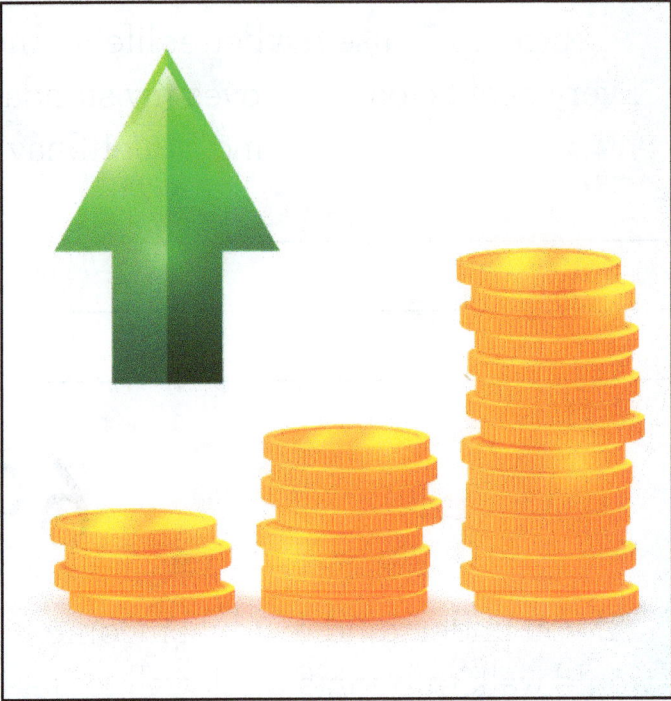

Section VI

Grow, Survive, and Thrive

There's no big hit when making money with residual income. You build up your income slowly. The benefit is that it just keeps on coming. Be passionate in what you do. Enjoy it. Stick with it, and over time, you will be pleasantly surprised at the value you create for your company and yourself.

70

Repeat sales are the way to financial freedom. @JeffShavitz

_____

_____

_____

71

Businesspeople who understand the power of compounding money will understand how money grows. And grows. And grows. @JeffShavitz

---

72

Building residual or passive income is a long-term project – this is not a "get rich quick" scheme! @JeffShavitz

---

73

Learn from mentors in a residual-based business what they did and what made them successful! No need to re-invent the wheel. @JeffShavitz

_____

_____

_____

74

Determine how many deals you should be closing each month to hit your goal; then do it. @JeffShavitz

_____

_____

_____

75

If you did a regression analysis, it should be going up and up with a good slope; otherwise, you're in the wrong business. @JeffShavitz

_____

_____

_____

76

A good residual salesperson should see their income growing in an ever-increasing direction, month after month. @JeffShavitz

_____

_____

_____

77

What is your breakeven point in paying a cancellation fee to obtain a new customer? You better know the answer. @JeffShavitz

_____

_____

_____

78

How much fun to receive
"mailbox money" every day of the year?
The money just appears. @JeffShavitz

_____

_____

_____

79

Figure out how to leverage yourself & your
time. Leverage is critical for growth.
@JeffShavitz

_____

_____

_____

80

It helps to stay motivated knowing that
this deal, this piece of work will
make your life better in a month.
@JeffShavitz

_____

_____

_____

81

Speak to customers: "Your most unhappy customers are your greatest source of learning." -Bill Gates, Microsoft co-founder. @JeffShavitz

_____

_____

_____

82

Create a mini sales org offering the same products; in essence, you become the franchisor and continue to grow. @JeffShavitz

_____

_____

_____

83

Everybody you know should know one potential customer; use your network of personal friends to grow your business. @JeffShavitz

_____

_____

_____

84

Get involved in your local business community; for one, it's the right thing to do & two, business partnerships will develop. @JeffShavitz

_____

_____

_____

85

Always understand the acquisition cost to develop a new client; you must know what that number is! @JeffShavitz

_____

_____

_____

86

Be creative in your marketing. Everybody does the "same stuff." You shouldn't. As the adage goes, "think outside the box." @JeffShavitz

_____

_____

_____

87

Offer equity very carefully to potential partners. Your residual business will be worth a lot of money in the future.
@JeffShavitz

_____

_____

_____

88

Speak for free at industry events, universities, chambers. It's a great way to meet local businesspeople. @JeffShavitz

_____

_____

_____

89

Attend tradeshows and conferences: great ways to nurture new relationships. @JeffShavitz

_____

_____

_____

90

Don't panic when you lose a customer.
Work hard to replace them. @JeffShavitz

_____

_____

_____

91

Don't take your residuals for granted.
@JeffShavitz

_____

_____

_____

92

Stay in touch with your customers and call in monthly to sleep well at night, or you will lose your valued accounts. @JeffShavitz

_____

_____

_____

93

Negotiate annual contracts so you know you're good for at least 12 months of income. @JeffShavitz

_____

_____

_____

94

Go after industries that lend themselves to residual payments. @JeffShavitz

_____

_____

_____

95

Be challenged to increase your residual income every pay period. Set a goal for an additional 5% per month. @JeffShavitz

_____

_____

_____

96

Of course, some deals will be more profitable than others. Know the difference. @JeffShavitz

_____

_____

_____

97

What's the worst thing a prospective client can say to you? "No." @JeffShavitz

_____

_____

_____

98

Offering a 30-day guarantee and a two-week free trial is a good incentive to have a client "test" your product. @JeffShavitz

_____

_____

_____

99

Use the word "educate" vs. "sell" when soliciting new prospects. If it's a good product/service, it will sell itself. @JeffShavitz

_____

_____

_____

100

Set a budget in writing in Jan., and continue to work your proformas monthly, quarterly & semi-annually to reach your goals. @JeffShavitz

_____

_____

_____

101

The "rich get richer while the poor get poorer." It's not fair, but important to learn how to grow wealth. @JeffShavitz

_____

_____

_____

102

Return on your time skyrockets when you have a solid customer base that buys from you month after month, year after year. @JeffShavitz

_____

_____

_____

103

Call 3 prospects or existing customers daily. At the end of the year, that's 900 people (assuming 300 work days). @JeffShavitz

_____

_____

_____

104

Ask family and friends for introductions to potential clients. You're doing the client a benefit by offering your service.
@JeffShavitz

_____

_____

_____

105

Having an initial "low teaser offer" providing great value is a great way to get a customer to try your product or service. @JeffShavitz

_____

_____

_____

106

"Work smarter, not harder" is a key truism
in a residual-based business model.
@JeffShavitz

_____

_____

_____

107

Create a financial sales proforma to highlight your earnings potential based on different assumptions. @JeffShavitz

_____

_____

_____

108

Make sure your plan is on paper.
Not just in your head. @JeffShavitz

_____

_____

_____

109

Find an industry that you can relate to &
combine your passion for selling with an
industry that makes sense to you.
@JeffShavitz

_____

_____

_____

110

The most important asset you have is your client. Never forget that. @JeffShavitz

_____

_____

_____

111

Yes, work hard, but taking a vacation is necessary to be successful. You need balance. @JeffShavitz

_____

_____

_____

112

Become an industry expert on a specific vertical niche – then identify a residual business in that sector. @JeffShavitz

---

113

Try to self-fund your company as long as possible. Interns are a great way to get started while money is tight. @JeffShavitz

---

114

Understand the training program and support systems when buying into a residual or MLM network marketing business. @JeffShavitz

_____

_____

_____

115

Strategic business partnerships are critical to growing your business. @JeffShavitz

_____

_____

_____

116

Find a mentor in network marketing to teach you. There are literally thousands of residual businesses to join. @JeffShavitz

_____

_____

_____

Section VII

Be Motivated!

You are on the right track. Take stock of who you are today and set a goal of where you and your company are heading. Keep moving forward. Stay motivated; you'll make it happen.

117

Have you read "Jeff Shavitz on Small Business AhaMessages"? I heard it's a must-read. http://aha.pub/smallbizahas @JeffShavitz

_____

_____

_____

118

Why didn't anyone tell me about the residual compensation model before I took a 9AM-5PM job with finite earnings? @JeffShavitz

_____

_____

_____

119

According to Forbes, the 400 wealthiest Americans have more wealth than the bottom 150 million Americans combined. @JeffShavitz

_____

_____

_____

120

Who is "the middle class" – are you? Are you the upper middle class? Are you rich? Poor? @JeffShavitz

_____

_____

_____

121

Have you saved money for your children's college tuition? Ancillary income helps, even if just a few hundred dollars per month. @JeffShavitz

_____

_____

_____

122

You must understand how much money each customer will generate in monthly earnings to you. @JeffShavitz

_____

_____

_____

123

A wise man told me years ago, "You want a raise? Then sell more." @JeffShavitz

_____

_____

_____

124

Congrats, you just gave yourself a raise,
be it $10 or $1,000 per month with
that new sale. @JeffShavitz

_____

_____

_____

125

What a thrill to close a new merchant account and know you just made money for the next 5-10 years. @JeffShavitz

---

126

Don't worry if you only earn $25,000 in your first year. It will grow quickly if you continue to work hard. @JeffShavitz

---

127

If you have a bad week or month, can you still pay the bills? Can you take off when you want, for as long as you want? @JeffShavitz

_____

_____

_____

128

True financial freedom is earning positive
cash flow from passive income.
You can do it! @JeffShavitz

_____

_____

_____

129

Making money while I slept really stuck
with me in comparison to people who I see
fighting for raises. @JeffShavitz

_____

_____

_____

130

Think about charging a monthly fee vs. an annual membership fee; it's easier to close the deal using this model. @JeffShavitz

_____

_____

_____

131

Continue to invest money and time to become a professional salesperson; otherwise, you'll be called an "empty suit." @JeffShavitz

_____

_____

_____

132

Study your monthly commission/residual
reports to understand if your customer is
buying more or less. Know your customer.
@JeffShavitz

_____

_____

_____

133

I love giving myself an annual bonus each
day that I close a new sale! @JeffShavitz

_____

_____

_____

134

I always feel confident that in the future,
I will be doing better. In one year from now,
I will be making more money.
@JeffShavitz

_____

_____

_____

135

"Time, perseverance & 10 years of trying will make you look like an overnight success."
-Biz Stone, Twitter co-founder via @JeffShavitz

_____

_____

_____

136

Good to feel nervous and anxious every day. Otherwise, you are not living and growing. @JeffShavitz

_____

_____

_____

137

"Insanity is doing the same thing over and over again and expecting different results."
-Albert Einstein via @JeffShavitz

_____

_____

_____

138

Watch your attrition. It's that important.
@JeffShavitz

_____

_____

_____

139

Have you read "Size Doesn't Matter:
Why Small Business Is BIG Business"?
I heard it's a great book. @JeffShavitz

_____

_____

_____

140

When was the last time you promoted yourself from "Salesman" to "Director of Sales?" Push yourself to sell. @JeffShavitz

_____

_____

_____

About the Author

Jeff Shavitz is a successful entrepreneur. He worked as an investment banker at Lehman Brothers in the Corporate Finance/Mergers and Acquisitions Group, specializing in transactions ranging from $250MM to $500MM. With an offer in hand to attend graduate school to earn his MBA and continue his climb up the corporate ladder, Jeff consciously decided to leave this fast-paced, well-paying position to start up a one-person business. Friends said, "What is he thinking?"

A passion for creating "a life of his own" was the driving force in determining Jeff's business future. Out of his New York apartment, while still working on Wall Street, he created "Spectoculars," a branded paper-folding binoculars that received an NFL license in 1991. At Super Bowl XXX, 250,000 pairs were distributed.

Fast-forward several years, and Jeff cofounded Charge Card Systems Inc., a national credit card processing company that helps merchants with their processing requirements, including the acceptance of Visa, MasterCard, American Express, and Discover. The company grew to more than 700 sales agents throughout the country with three regional offices. In 2012, Jeff and his partners sold the business to Card Connect, owned by private equity firm FTV Capital. The purchase was the company's largest acquisition to date.

The culmination of Jeff's past experiences with the small and mid-size business owners is TrafficJamming, LLC (www.trafficjamming.com), a membership association for business owners and entrepreneurs. All businesses want more traffic—in essence, traffic means sales. TrafficJamming provides its members with a destination website filled with information, technology tools, and insights to help grow your business. TrafficJamming is not a buying club or traditional business group, but rather, a modern organization to help executives realize their professional dreams. Among its many services, TrafficJamming provides proven and cutting-edge technology solutions to help build awareness of our members' products and services—with the ultimate goal of building a loyal tribe of clients.

In addition to *Jeff Shavitz on The Power of Residual Income: You Can Bank On It*, Jeff has also published the following books:

– *Size Doesn't Matter: Why Small Business Is BIG Business*, which hit #1 on the Amazon new releases in Entrepreneurship. In this book, Jeff details his personal and professional experiences, observations, challenges, and rewards in operating small businesses.

– *Jeff Shavitz on Small Business AhaMessages™: 140 Key Axioms That Every Business Owner Should Consider*, a collection of 140 key axioms that every business owner should consider when starting or running their companies.

– *Jeff Shavitz on Networking: Get Connected*, a collection of 140 AHAmessages that discusses the most effective ways to nurture business relationships. Jeff has developed a philosophy that networking involves "Return on Time" (ROT)— using time properly to develop trusted and authentic relationships to help grow your company.

Jeff received his Bachelor of Arts degree in Economics from Tufts University and spent one semester at the London School of Economics, specializing in finance. He is very active in numerous charitable and civic community organizations and business groups, including Young Presidents' Organization.

He is married and has two daughters, a son, and two dogs. Besides being with family, enjoying good health, and living to see worldwide peace, Jeff's selfish goal is to play the 100 top golf courses in the United States.

To learn more about the author and his business, visit www.trafficjamming.com or contact him at jeff@trafficjamming.com and 800-878-4100.

AHAthat™

AHAthat™ is the only thought leadership platform with a built-in marketplace, making it easy to share curated content from like-minded thought leaders. There are over 30,000 diverse AHAmessages™ from thought leaders around the world.

AHAthat makes it easy to create, organize, and share your own thought leadership AHAmessages in digestible, bite-sized morsels. You can now easily "SHARE" other people's content in minutes, "AUTHOR" your own book in hours, and "PROMOTE" what you're doing directly to your fans/advocates through their networks.

The experience of many authors is that they have been able to create their social media-enabled AHAbook™ of 140 AHAmessages in eight to ten hours.

Sign up for a free account at
http://AHAthat.com today!

Please pick up a copy of this book on AHAthat
and share each AHAmessage socially at
http://aha.pub/residualincome.

www.ingramcontent.com/pod-product-compliance
Lightning Source LLC
Chambersburg PA
CBHW071217200326
41519CB00018B/5569